ABUELA'S WEAVE

BY OMAR S. CASTAÑEDA

ILLUSTRATED BY ENRIQUE O. SANCHEZ

LEE & LOW BOOKS Inc.
New York

Manufactured in China

Book Design by Christy Hale
Book Production by The Kids at Out House
The text is set in Meridien Medium
The illustrations are rendered in acrylic on canvas

(HC) 15 14 13 12 11
(PB) 20 19 18 17 16 15 14
First Edition

Library of Congress Cataloging-in-Publicatin Data
Castañeda, Omar S.
Abuela's Weave / by Omar S. Castañeda; illustated by Enrique O. Sanchez
p. cm.
Summary: A young Guatemalan girl and her grandmother grow closer
as they weave some special creations and then make a trip
to the market in hopes of selling them.
ISBN 1-880000-00-8 (hardcover)   ISBN 1-880000-20-2 (paperback)
[1. Guatemala—Fiction. 2. Grandmothers—Fiction.]
I. Sanchez, Enrique O., ill. II. Title.
PZ7.C26859Ab 1993
[E]—dc20   92-71927   CIP AC

Free Teacher's Guide available at leeandlow.com/teachers

*To my children, Omar and Bleu
and to my nephews and nieces,
Jason, Deanna, Hector, Delia
and Evahn Figueroa—O.S.C.*

To my son, Aron—E.O.S.

"Pull back hard," old Abuela said. "Make it jolt, so the threads stay close, like family."

"Yes, Abuela."

Esperanza thrust the bolt through the opened weave and pulled the bar down with all her might.

Next to her, Esperanza's grandmother, her Abuela, also kneeled in front of a backstrap loom. Both looms were tied to the same tree in the middle of the family compound. Esperanza's mother fed the chickens and pigs behind the main thatch hut while her father was off with her brothers in the field of corn, beans and coffee.

"You're learning," Abuela said.

Esperanza looked at her grandmother out of the corner of her eye. She knew that Abuela was nervous about the market. Her mother said that the *huipiles* and tapestries Abuela made could "pull the wonder right out of people." But these days, more and more goods were made by machines.

Esperanza worried that people would tease Abuela about her birthmark, as some kids had once done. They had started a rumor that she was a witch, and now many people were frightened to buy things from her.

"Daydreaming again?" Abuela asked.

"Yes, Abuela."

"Well," the old woman said gruffly, "get busy because there are too few days left. You still have a lot of work to do and there will be many other people selling the same things you have."

"Don't worry, Abuela, I'll be busy until we leave!"

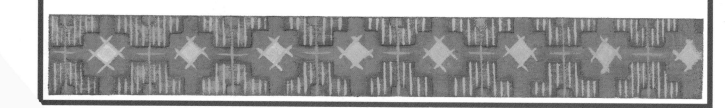

And she was. Esperanza and her grandmother worked from early morning, even before the sun rose, to well past sunset, when the moon rose and the compound fire gave everything the rich smell of pine.

They showed no one their work, not even Esperanza's mother, because it was a special thing that they wove. They wanted to wait for the Fiesta de Pueblos in Guate to reveal it.

Soon the day arrived. Bright with sun, the leaves glistening from the previous night's rain, it seemed like a good omen for Esperanza and her grandmother. Abuela appeared disguised as a woman in mourning. Dressed in black, she wrapped a long black shawl around her shoulders and across her face so that only her eyes appeared to the world.

Esperanza, however, wore her favorite *huipil*: it was a white blouse with red, blue and green threads in the rectangular collar. Under that, the colors bled into silver and blue, and hidden within the intricate designs of the blouse were tiny quetzals flying freely in the threads the way they once flew in the great forests of Guatemala.

She carried on her head a large straw basket full of her *huipiles,* tablecloths, skirts and the special tapestry.

Esperanza walked steadily down the dirt avenue of Santa Cruz to get to the highway where the Guate bus would pick them up. Abuela walked several paces behind. She insisted that they pretend they did not know each other.

"This way if my birthmark frightens customers, they will still buy from *you*,"Abuela explained.

When the bus came, Abuela did not even help lift the heavy basket to the boys who strapped bags onto the roof of the bus.

Inside, they sat three seats apart, as if they were strangers, people living in different villages, people with no ancestors in common.

When they arrived, the noise in the city was deafening. Large buses roared down the narrow streets, emitting clouds of black fumes. Horns blasted, and people hurried roughly down the sidewalks. Esperanza wanted more than anything to get off the Sexta Avenida where people jammed the walkways and hawkers yelled from their shops or from the hundreds of carts blocking the sidewalks and streets. She felt trapped. Her lungs ached from the automobile and bus fumes, and her ears rang with the sounds of screeching brakes, horns, shouting and the whistles of policemen.

Esperanza walked quickly, the basket steady upon her head, her mind trying to focus away from the commotion and onto the stalls set up for the fiesta in the Parque Central.

She walked furiously, zig-zagging to get down to Avenida Ocho or the Séptima Avenida, where the noise was less, when she suddenly stopped to see if Abuela was still following behind. She looked for a familiar face among the bobbing heads, the baskets, the helmets and hats. She wanted to catch just a sight of her grandmother's shawl, like a blackbird hopping from branch to branch in a forest of people, but she could not find her. Esperanza continued to the market, hoping Abuela would eventually find her there among the other merchants.

The stalls were already filled when Esperanza arrived. Old men and women nearby shooed her away or ignored her when she asked for help.

At last, all she could do was set her basket between the narrow slats of two stalls. On one side, a family from Antigua sold pottery, reproductions of Mayan crafts, and clothing loomed in one of the many factories.

The woman on the other side sold long bolts of cloth, musical instruments and decorative bags. The bags all had zippers machined in the capital and long handles of colorful plastic.

Everything was beautiful, Esperanza thought. She thought that no one would buy anything from her. She and her grandmother would return to Santa Cruz with no money, the long hours wasted, and the family disappointed.

Esperanza sadly took out her wares to hang them one by one on long splinters in the slat-wood on either side. She felt terribly alone. Even her poor Abuelita was nowhere to be seen.

The people slowly noticed. They pointed at the elaborate weaving.
Tourists and Guatemalans alike drew closer to her tiny place and
looked up with wonder at the beautiful work in front of them.

The large tapestry blossomed with images of Guatemala. Esperanza and Abuela had worked in intricate symbols of the country's history. There were heroines and heroes inspired by the glorious *Popol Vuh,* the sacred book of the Maya. And in one corner, a beautiful quetzal seemed to watch over it all from within a white cage.

In Esperanza's hands the tapestry's colors shone as brightly as the sun over Guatemala's Lake Atitlán.

People turned from the commercial stalls to stand before Esperanza's complex weaving. When she looked up, Esperanza saw Abuela with a smile across her birthmarked face.

It didn't take long for all of their work to be sold that day. The people were disappointed when all was gone, but Esperanza promised to return with new things the following month.

And on the way back to Santa Cruz, grandmother and granddaughter sat side by side, Esperanza's smooth and nimble fingers held tightly in her Abuela's wrinkled old hands.